From
Windmil...
Hydrogen ...

Discovering Alternative Energy
Sally Morgan

Heinemann Library
Chicago, Illinois

Customer Service 888-454-2279
Visit our website at www.heinemannraintree.com

For information, address the publisher:
Heinemann Library, 100 N. LaSalle, Suite 1200,
Chicago, IL 60602

Designed by Tim Mayer
Printed and bound in China by Leo Paper Group Ltd

11 10 09 08
10 9 8 7 6 5 4 3 2 1

Library of Congress Cataloging-in-Publication Data
Morgan, Sally.
    From windmills to hydrogen fuel cells : discovering
alternative energy / Sally Morgan.
        p. cm. -- (Chain reactions)
    ISBN 978-1-4034-9555-6 (hb)
    ISBN 978-1-4329-0709-9 (pb)
    1. Renewable energy sources--Juvenile literature. I.
Title.
    TJ808.2.M674 2007
    621.042--dc22

                                2006046853

Acknowledgements. The author and publisher would like
to thank the following for allowing their pictures to be
reproduced in this publication: Corbis pp. 4 (Bojan
Brecelj), 12–13 (Owaki - Kulla), 19 (Bettmann), 36
(Bettmann), 37 (David Nicholls), 41 (Reuters), 43 (Hubert
Stadler), 44–45 (Charles and Josette Lenars), 55
(Andrew Wong/Reuters); Digital Vision p. 20;
Ecoscene pp. 7 (Bruce Harber), 11 (Graham Kitching),
14–15 (Jim Winkley), 17 (Jim Winkley); Getty Images
pp. 46 (Robert Nickelsberg/Time Life), 49 (Andre
Vieira); Index Stock Imagery/Photolibrary pp. 21, 22,
30; iStockphoto.com pp. 1 (Aravind Teki), 29 (Craig
Shanklin), 48 (Aravind Teki); Monsoonimages/
Photolibrary p. 8; NASA p. 52; Ocean Power Delivery
Ltd, 104 Commercial Street, Edinburgh EH6 6NF,
United Kingdom p. 34); Phototake Inc/Photolibrary
p. 25; Science Photo Library pp. 24 (Detlev van
Ravenswaay), 27 (Adam Hart-Davis), 28, 32 (Martin
Bond), 33 (Martin Bond), 42 (Klaus Guldbrandsen), 50
(Pasquale Sorrentino), 51 (Martin Bond); TopFoto.co.uk
pp. 16 (Boyer/Roger-Viollet), 38 (Topham), 47 (Topham).

Cover design by Tim Mayer.

Disclaimer
All the Internet addresses (URLs) given in this book were
valid at the time of going to press. However, due to the
dynamic nature of the Internet, some addresses may
have changed, or sites may have ceased to exist since
publication. While the author and publishers regret any
inconvenience this may cause readers, no responsibility
for any such changes can be accepted by either the
author or the publishers.

Contents

Any words appearing in the text in bold, **like this**, are explained in the Glossary.

Fossil Fuels versus New Fuels

Imagine a time 50 years into the future. Europe and North America have just experienced some of the worst winter storms in living memory. Newspaper headlines announce that oil and gas supplies are at an all-time low. Power stations are short of fuel, and power outages happen every day. The streets are dark at night, as the lighting has been switched off. There are lines at the gas stations, as desperate motorists wait for their tiny ration of gasoline.

This may seem far-fetched, but it could happen if the world continues to rely on coal, oil, and gas to supply electricity and fuel vehicles. Today's society is energy-hungry. We use electricity to power computers, washing machines, air conditioning units, and many other electrical appliances.

Fossil fuels

Fossil fuels—oil, gas, and coal—currently generate most of the world's electricity. These fuels are derived from living organisms that died millions of years ago. However, fossil fuel reserves are limited. As demand increases, especially in newly industrialized countries such as China and India, these reserves are fast running out. In the coming 100 years, the world's demand for energy is likely to more than double. Experts estimate that the world's known oil and gas reserves will last between 30 and 60 years, while coal might last about 200 years.

THAT'S AMAZING!

In 2004, world energy consumption rose by 4.3 percent, the largest-ever increase in energy consumption in one year.

New fuels

We urgently need to make greater use of renewable energies, such as solar, wind, and wave power. There have already been some "wake-up calls." In the 1970s, there was an energy crisis as a result of war and political instability in the Middle East. Oil supplies were reduced and prices soared. This forced many countries to look seriously at using alternatives, such as wind power and solar energy. In the United States, the first commercial wind farms and solar power stations appeared. In 2005, continuing instability in the oil-producing nations pushed oil prices to record levels. This put economic growth at risk in the rest of the world.

The other big reason to move away from fossil fuels is **climate change**. When coal, oil, and gas are burned to generate heat in power stations, vast quantities of carbon dioxide are released. Carbon dioxide is one of the main **greenhouse gases** that contribute to **global warming**. As more fossil fuels are burned, more carbon dioxide is produced. In 2005, carbon dioxide levels in the atmosphere reached a record high. The levels have to be lowered if the consequences of global warming, such as climate change, rising sea levels, and more extreme weather, are to be avoided.

This is an industrial zone in Shanghai, China. Coal generates more than 65 percent of China's energy. China's oil consumption is expected to rise from 6.5 million barrels per day to 14.2 million barrels per day by 2025.

Tackling the problem of climate change

Most power stations are powered by fossil fuels, so if people and industry use less electricity, fewer fossil fuels need to be burned. Power stations can be made more efficient. They will then produce more electricity for each ton of fuel. Using vehicles less also helps. However, switching to cleaner energy sources, both for generating electricity and powering vehicles, is likely to have the greatest impact.

The history of alternative fuels

People have used a variety of energy sources for hundreds of years. For instance, they have used water power to grind grain and wind and horse power to pump water. But most of the main technological breakthroughs were made in the late 1700s and early 1800s, when inventors were developing better ways of harnessing these energy sources.

This chart shows the energy sources that were used to generate the world's electricity in 2005.

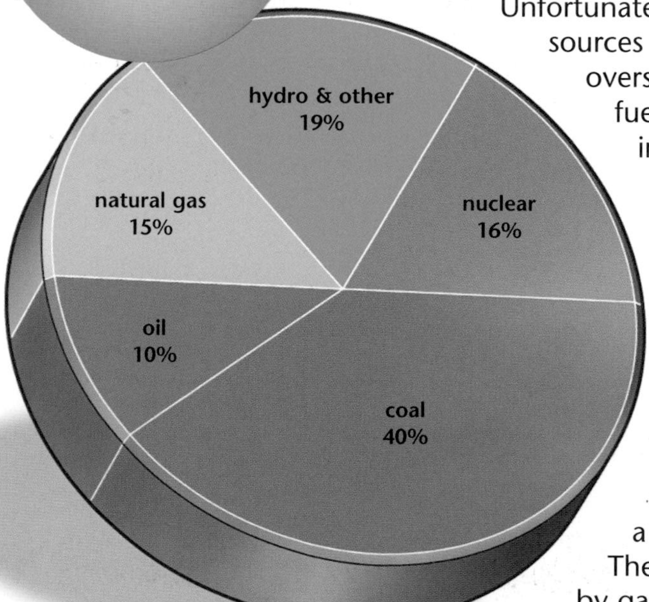

hydro & other
19%

natural gas
15%

nuclear
16%

oil
10%

coal
40%

Unfortunately, alternative energy sources have always been overshadowed by fossil fuels. This pattern started in the 1760s, when Scottish inventor James Watt (1736–1819) modified the steam engine, which was powered by coal. In the 1880s, coal and water power were the first sources of energy used to make electricity on a commercial scale. These were followed by gas and oil. Fossil fuels soon became the main energy source because they were cheap and plentiful. Nuclear energy appeared after World War Two (1939–1945) but the other sources of energy were virtually ignored until very recently.

Combining energy sources

This book looks at the different alternative energy sources, how they have been developed, and how they could supply electricity in the future. Each energy source has its own story, some dating back thousands of years. No single alternative energy source will be able to replace fossil fuels. Instead, a mix of many different sources will be required, such as nuclear, wind, and solar power.

In Denmark, eco-friendly houses are already being built. This house in the village of Torup Eco has its own wind-power generator, and its dome shape reduces heat loss by about 30 percent.

This book shows how the different energy sources can be developed commercially and the ways in which they can be used together. For example, the home of the future could have solar panels and a small wind **turbine** on the roof. The boiler would perhaps be replaced by a hydrogen-powered **fuel cell** to generate electricity, while the waste heat would be used to heat water. The car would also be powered by a fuel cell.

A hundred years ago, many pioneering scientists working on wind and solar power warned that one day the world would run out of oil and coal. Their warnings were ignored. Now the scientists and the energy companies have to race to develop new energy sources before the oil wells dry up.

Wind Power

One of the most popular alternative energy sources is wind power. Strong winds occur all over the world, and most countries have suitable sites on which to build wind **turbines**. This source of energy could potentially supply 1.5 percent of the world's electricity by 2010. As the costs come down, this percentage could rise. Denmark already generates about 10 percent of its electricity using wind power. In the future, the vast windswept plains of Mongolia could become a major source of wind power for the world.

The inspiration for the first wind machines built in Persia, in about 500 B.C.E, came from the sails used on boats. These early wind machines had sails that caught the wind and turned a millstone to grind grain. By C.E. 1000, wind machines had become more powerful. They were particularly common in China and the eastern Mediterranean, where they were used to pump water.

Over the years, more than 6 million mechanical wind pumps for pumping water have been constructed in the United States. This one is in Noble Springs, Nevada. There are millions more elsewhere in the world.

The sails were a triangular shape, which was good for catching the wind. They were attached to a vertical shaft, which was connected to a grinding stone. This design became very common throughout Europe until about 1800.

Wind pumps

During the 1800s, settlers moved into the drier areas of North America and built thousands of wind pumps to pump water from the ground. The most popular was the Halladay windmill, designed in 1854. This windmill had four wooden paddle-like blades attached to a wooden tower. In 1870, steel blades arrived. Steel was lighter and could be cut into more **aerodynamic** shapes, so these blades were more efficient.

Generating electricity

Electricity became common in the late 1800s. Most electricity was generated using energy from coal, wood, or water. Now engineers wanted to see if they could generate electricity using wind power.

The first large windmill to generate electricity was the Brush Machine in Cleveland, Ohio. It was built in 1888 by Charles F. Brush. Its **rotor** had many blades and was 56 feet (17 meters) in diameter. The Brush Machine was also the first to have a gearbox to control the speed at which the blades rotated. This wind machine generated 12 **kilowatts** of electricity. At the time, this was considered a lot. However, a modern wind machine can generate as much as 100 kilowatts. Later windmills had even more blades, and they could turn in order to catch the wind.

THAT'S AMAZING!

As wind turbines got larger in the late 1800s, they were more prone to wind damage. Some of the more advanced designs had blades that could fold up like an umbrella to prevent damage when there were high winds.

Wind turbines in the 1900s

By World War One (1914–1918), wind turbines were being built with longer blades, and they were generating more power. One of the largest experimental machines was the Palmer-Putnam machine. This was built in the United States in the 1930s. It had 164-foot (50-meter) diameter rotors and it could generate 1.25 **megawatts** of electricity. But this type of turbine was made using heavy materials that reduced its efficiency.

World War Two (1939–1945) stopped research on wind turbines, but it started again in the 1950s. One of the most influential designs was the Gedser wind turbine, built in 1956–1957 by Johannes Juul in Denmark. This had a horizontal axis and three blades, and it could generate an amazing 200 kilowatts.

Many turbine engineers looked to aeroplane technology for ideas. Aeronautical engineers use lightweight materials such as aluminium. They also incorporate hollow structures in their designs, as they give more strength for less weight. In the 1960s, a German named Professor Ulrich Hutter made blades from lightweight materials such as fiberglass and plastic. These materials were relatively cheap, and they allowed the rotors to be turned by light winds. By 1986, turbines could generate as much as 600 kilowatts, due to improved blade design and the use of lightweight materials.

This diagram shows the inside of a wind turbine.

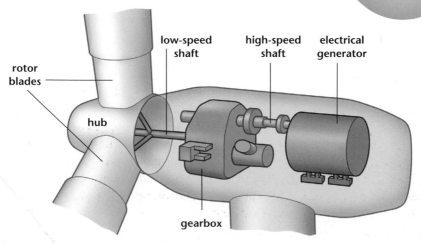

rotor blades

hub

low-speed shaft

high-speed shaft

electrical generator

gearbox

Modern Darrieus turbines (see panel below) have four curved blades that revolve around a vertical tube. They work equally well regardless of the wind direction. They are secured by ropes to prevent damage in high winds.

A 600-kilowatt turbine has blades up to 164 feet (50 meters) long. But stronger winds are needed to turn the longer blades, and few sites have strong winds all year round. Most wind turbines are therefore designed to generate about 55 kilowatts.

The majority of modern wind turbines are Horizontal Axis Wind Turbines (HAWTs). They have a propeller-type rotor attached to a horizontal main shaft. The rotor converts the energy of the moving air into mechanical energy, which drives a generator. The rotor blades are connected to the hub. When the wind is too strong, the brakes stop the blades from turning too quickly.

WHAT WAS THE DARRIEUS DESIGN?

Frenchman G.J.M. Darrieus patented his Vertical Axis Wind Turbine (VAWT) in 1931. His rotor had three slender curved blades. These were attached, top and bottom, to a rotating vertical tube. It looked a bit like a giant egg-beater! This design did not need a tower, and the gearbox and generator were on the ground so they were easier to maintain. However, it was not as efficient as a HAWT because wind speed is lower nearer the ground. This design was overlooked until the 1960s, when Canadian engineers rediscovered the patent and built their own Darrieus wind turbine.

Blade design

A wind turbine blade has to extract as much energy as possible from the wind. It also has to be cheap, durable, and quiet. A blade is a similar shape to the wing of a plane. A poorly designed blade will not move through the air cleanly. Instead, it creates drag. This slows down the speed of the blade and generates more noise. Drag can be reduced by making the surface very smooth.

The growth of wind farms

Although wind turbines gradually became more efficient, they could not compete with the cost of electricity generated using fossil fuels. However, the oil crisis of the 1970s changed everything. Soon, large wind farms were being constructed in Denmark and also in California. The U.S. government encouraged the growth and development of wind farms by changing tax laws.

The oil crisis started in October 1973, when Arab members of the Organization of Petroleum Exporting Countries (OPEC) announced that they would no longer ship oil to countries that supported Israel in its war with Syria and Egypt. This meant the supply of oil to the United States and parts of Europe slowed down. At the same time, OPEC decided to increase the cost of oil four-fold. Although the crisis was resolved by March 1974, western economies had been severely affected, and western governments decided they had to reduce their dependence on Middle Eastern oil.

This wind farm is in California. The layout of a wind farm is very important, as the individual turbines create areas of turbulence. Engineers use computer programs to analyze the flow of air through the wind farm and figure out the ideal layout for maximum efficiency.

Between 1981 and 1990, more than 17,000 turbines were constructed in the United States. However, these early wind farms were poorly designed, and their maintenance costs were high. In 1984–1985, the tax laws changed, and the market for wind energy disappeared overnight. By 1990, only a few wind farms were being installed. But wind power remained popular in Europe, especially in Denmark and Germany.

An alternative to oil?

Wind power is more popular today because it is a renewable energy source. In addition, it does not create air pollution, unlike fossil fuel–fired power stations. Many countries have agreed to cut their carbon dioxide **emissions** in order to combat **global warming**. Wind power could help them achieve their targets.

The cost of oil and gas has continued to rise over the last 30 years. Although coal is still available, it is less efficient than oil and gas. It also produces more air pollution. During the same period, the cost per kilowatt hour of electricity generated by wind power has dropped by about 50 percent. In addition, the cost of building the turbines has fallen. This means that it could be cheaper to install a wind farm than to build a small power station.

Going offshore

There are a limited number of sites where wind farms can be built on land. And local residents often object to their construction because they scar the landscape and generate noise and flickering lights. However, strong winds are common at sea, so engineers started to design wind turbines that could be placed offshore. In 1990, the world's first experimental offshore wind turbine was built 820 feet (250 meters) off the coast of Sweden. A year later, construction started on the first commercial offshore wind farm of 11 turbines in the Baltic Sea, off the Danish coast.

An offshore location offered several benefits, particularly stronger and more constant winds. However, there were technical hurdles to overcome. For example, they had to design a turbine that could withstand strong currents and breaking waves. Ice was a problem too, and cones were placed around the turbine at water level to act as ice breakers.

This offshore wind farm is located outside Copenhagen Harbor, in Denmark.

In 2005, the world's biggest offshore wind farm was Denmark's Nysted wind farm, which produces up to 165 megawatts.

There are plans for many more wind farms around the world. In England, there is a proposal to build 270 wind turbines in the Thames Estuary. These are expected to generate up to 1,000 megawatts (1 **gigawatt**) of renewable energy by 2011, enough to power 25 percent of London homes.

The future of wind power

Wind turbines seem to be developing in several directions. At one end of the scale, larger turbines, suited to offshore wind farms or windy places, are being built. However, there is also a growing demand for small turbines to power remote villages in developing countries. In addition, there are micro turbines that can be fixed to the roofs of houses to supply enough electricity to power lights.

Ocean currents are common off many coasts, and the energy of the moving water can be harnessed to generate electricity in the same way as wind (moving air) is harnessed by a wind turbine. One design is the tidal turbine. It looks just like a wind turbine, but the blades are under water and they are moved by water currents.

HOW MUCH ELECTRICITY DOES WIND POWER GENERATE?

By the end of 2004, the world's wind turbines were able to generate almost 48 gigawatts (about 0.6 percent of the world's electricity). Experts have predicted that this could rise to 117 gigawatts by 2009. This may seem a lot, but it is still only 1.5 percent of the total world usage. However, the figure could increase if more countries invest in new wind technology. Countries with the largest installed wind power capacity are: Germany (18,440 megawatts), Spain (10,030 megawatts), the United States (9,150 megawatts), India (4,430 megawatts), and Denmark (3,120 megawatts).

Solar Energy

Wind power has been used for thousands of years, but solar power is a more recent development. Over the last 60 years, technological advances have resulted in solar power being used in many more ways.

Horace de Saussure built his model greenhouses because he wanted to find out how much heat could be trapped by glass.

Hot boxes

In 1767, Horace de Saussure (1740–1799), a Swiss scientist, built some tiny model greenhouses, each one smaller than the last. He stacked them, one inside the other, and left them on a black wooden table in the sun. After several hours, he measured the temperature inside. It had reached 189.5 °Fahrenheit (87.5 °Celsius). Next, he made a small wooden box and lined it with black cork. He covered the top of the box with three sheets of glass and found that the temperature inside then soared to 228 °Fahrenheit (109 °Celsius). He called this device a "hot box" because it retained so much heat. This invention was the first in a chain that led to modern solar panels used on roofs.

? WHY DOES IT GET HOT IN A GREENHOUSE?

Sunlight passes through the panes of glass and is absorbed by the plants and surfaces inside. Light energy is converted into heat energy. The heat is released and the air warms up. The glass does not allow the heat to escape, so it remains trapped inside.

The solar water heater

The hot box idea was taken further by American inventor Clarence Kemp, who designed a solar water heater. He patented his design in 1891 and called it the Climax solar heater. It consisted of four cylindrical water tanks in a wooden box, lined with felt, and covered with a pane of glass. The box was placed in a sunny position on the roof. Cold water was piped into the first tank. As the water circulated, it heated up. Hot water was then piped out of the last tank. By 1900, more than 1,600 Climax units had been sold.

Today, solar heating panels are commonly placed on the roofs of houses in sunny countries, such as Spain, Greece, and Israel. The sunlight passes through a glass panel and heats the liquid flowing through the pipes inside the panel. The hot liquid from the solar panel is pumped to the domestic water tank. It then flows through a coiled pipe, called a heat exchanger. Here, heat from the hot liquid in the pipes is transferred to the water in the tank. Then the liquid is pumped back to the roof, to be heated again.

This solar heating panel, on the roof of a house in the Canary Islands, uses energy from the sun to provide hot water for the household.

The first solar motor

During the 1760s, Scotsman James Watt had modified the steam engine, which used coal to generate steam, to power a machine. Frenchman Auguste Mouchout wanted to use the sun's heat to produce steam. In 1860, he came up with a design for a solar-powered motor. It was a water-filled iron pot inside a glass frame. The sunlight passed through the glass and was converted into heat. The iron pot absorbed the heat. The water in the pot then came to a boil and produced steam.

At first, the device did not produce enough steam, so Mouchout added a huge dish-shaped reflector. This focused the sunlight directly onto the pot. Finally, he designed a mechanism to track the sun as it moved across the sky. This succeeded, and he was then sent to Algeria to build a solar engine that could pump water. He achieved this using several boilers to increase the engine's performance. However, the price of coal was falling. It therefore became cheaper to burn coal than to build complicated solar-powered machines.

The parabolic trough

Swedish inventor John Ericsson (1803–1889) was working in the United States during the late 1800s. He was convinced that coal supplies would run out and that people would need to harness the sun's energy.

WHAT IS A POWER TOWER?

Mouchout's steam-powered engine inspired other people, including William Adams, an Englishman working in Bombay, India. In 1878, Adams built his alternative to the reflector dish—the **power tower**. He used rows of small, flat mirrors on a rack. This rack rolled around a semicircular track, reflecting sunlight onto a boiler. His tower could power a 2.5 **horsepower** steam engine. Although it attracted a lot of interest, it could not compete with coal or wood. However, Adams' design was not forgotten. One hundred years later, it formed the basis of the world's first large-scale solar power plant in California.

In 1870, Ericsson built his first solar-powered steam engine. This used a dish-shaped reflector and a tracking mechanism that were similar to those made by Mouchout.

Then, during the 1880s, Ericsson designed the **parabolic trough**. This resembles an oil drum cut in half, with a reflective surface on the inside. The reflector focuses the sunlight onto a pipe carrying a fluid. The temperature of the fluid increases as it flows through the pipe. Ericsson's parabolic trough was much cheaper to make than the dish-shaped reflector designed by Mouchout. However, the troughs could not generate temperatures as high as those produced by the dish-shaped reflectors. Ericsson died before he could mass-produce his system. But, just like the power tower, the parabolic trough would later become popular with engineers working on solar power in the 1970s.

This illustration shows Ericsson's solar engine with its huge parabolic trough.

Solar power stations

In 1912, American Frank Shuman built a solar pumping station in Egypt, using rows of parabolic reflectors. The steam operated an engine that pumped water. This proved that it was possible to use solar power on a large scale. However, within two years the plant had been destroyed in World War One (1914–1918). Interest in Shuman's solar plant ended with his death a couple of years later. It then took about 50 years before the world's first solar power station was built.

The huge reflector at Odeillo, France, is made up of 9,500 mirrors. These mirrors concentrate the Sun's rays on to a furnace in the central tower.

The next generation of solar power engineers studied the designs of the past, analyzing their performance, cost, and reliability. Dish-shaped reflectors were found to be the most efficient but also the most difficult to maintain. Power towers and parabolic reflectors, although less efficient, were considered better options overall, as they were easier to build and maintain.

During the 1960s, French engineers constructed a solar power station in Odeillo, France. This had a parabolic reflector that reflected light onto a central tower. The energy was used to power a furnace that produced steel from iron ore. The engineers placed 63 **heliostats** (small mirrors) on terraces opposite, to increase the light falling on the main reflector. The Odeillo solar power station is still in use today.

THAT'S AMAZING!

In 1775, French chemist Antoine Lavoisier (1743–1794) built a solar furnace that reached 3,236 °Fahrenheit (1,780 °Celsius). At this temperature, the metal platinum would melt.

The oil crisis of the 1970s stimulated investment in solar energy in the United States. Solar One, near Barstow, California, was a power tower, which operated from 1982 to 1988. Its capacity was around 10 **megawatts**. It was surrounded by about 1,800 small heliostats that reflected light onto the top of the central tower. The light raised the temperature to produce steam, which was used to drive a steam **turbine**. In 1996, Solar Two, using more advanced technology, started operating.

The power towers were not the only solar plants in California. The Luz Engineering Corporation built 10 solar plants in the Mojave desert. These used parabolic trough reflectors to drive steam-powered turbines. The largest plant was capable of generating around 80 megawatts.

A number of solar power stations are currently being planned. There is a proposal to build the world's largest solar power station in southern Portugal. It would cover 600 acres (250 hectares) and have an output of about 116 megawatts (enough to power 130,000 homes). It would be so large that it could be seen from space. A 15-megawatt solar power station is under construction in South Korea. Meanwhile, in Israel, plans are being drawn up to build a 100-megawatt solar power station in the Negev desert.

Lines of parabolic trough reflectors in the Mojave desert, in California, collect solar energy.

This solar-powered portable traffic signal can be used in very remote locations.

Photovoltaics

Research into solar power has followed two paths. One path focuses on converting sunlight to produce heat for heating systems or making steam to generate electricity. The second looks at ways of turning sunlight directly into electricity.

In the 1800s, Alexandre-Edmond Becquerel, a French physicist, was experimenting with a process called **electrolysis** (see page 50). In this process, an electric current is passed through a solution called an **electrolyte**. In 1839, Becquerel placed an **electrode** in an electrolyte. He then noticed that a small electric current was produced when the electrode was exposed to light. This was the photovoltaic effect—the conversion of light into electricity. He reported this in a scientific paper, but did not follow up the experiment with any further research.

The first solar cell

In 1883, American inventor Charles Fritts was working with selenium, a metallic substance that can conduct electricity under certain conditions. Fritts had coated a piece of selenium with a very thin layer of gold. When he placed it in sunlight, he managed to generate a small electric current. He had made the first solar cell. It was not very efficient, as only 1 percent of the light falling on the cell was converted into electricity. But it was a start.

HOW ARE PV CELLS USED?

PV cells are used around the world in many different ways. For example, they are used to provide electricity in remote locations, to power road signs and marine buoys, and to power hand-held calculators. They have also been used in space, where they power satellites and space shuttles.

About 50 years later, American scientist Russell Ohl was investigating ways of producing pure silicon crystals that could be used in radios. One afternoon in 1939, he noticed that when a light shone on a particular crystal of silicon, a small electrical current was produced. On further examination, he saw that the crystal had a crack down the middle. Ohl thought the crack must have formed because of impurities in the crystal. When light shone on the crystal, the **electrons** (negatively charged particles) moved around. But they were unable to cross the crack, and this generated a small electric current. Ohl concluded that the presence of the crack was causing the electrons to move in the same direction, thus producing an electrical current. His work helped explain how silicon crystals could be used to generate electrical currents.

The next step forward was taken by three American researchers, Gerald Pearson, Calvin Fuller, and Daryl Chapin, who were working for Bell Telephone Laboratories. In 1954, they designed the first **photovoltaic (PV) cell**. They placed several small strips of silicon in sunlight and generated an electric current. Their simple PV cell could convert 6 percent of the sunlight into electricity. Further improvements in the design increased this to 11 percent. Nowadays PV cells are about 17 percent efficient. With further refinements, it might even be possible to achieve 50 percent efficiency.

A space power station

Ever since 1958, PV cells have been used to power satellites, spacecraft, and space shuttles. The first was the *Vanguard I* satellite, which had a small photovoltaic array to power its radio. The PV cells had to be treated in order to resist the radiation that would bombard them in space.

This illustration shows how a future solar power station might work. Large arrays of solar panels convert the sun's energy into microwaves. A beam of microwaves transfers energy to the southwestern United States. The control center of the solar power satellite is being serviced by a spacecraft.

After the 1970s oil crisis, the National Aeronautics and Space Administration (NASA) started carrying out research into the use of solar power in space. The clouds and dust in the atmosphere reduce the amount of sunlight reaching Earth's surface. As a result, there is more than 8 times more sunlight in space, and it is available 24 hours a day.

solar panels

microwaves

service spacecraft

One of the designs under consideration is a giant orbiting solar power station, which would be covered in PV cells. However, there are many technical challenges to overcome. One suggestion is to convert the electricity into **microwaves**. The microwaves could be transmitted to Earth and then be converted back into electricity.

◗◗ TALKING SCIENCE

"With funding and support, we can continue developing this technology. We offer an advantage. You don't need cables, pipes, gas, or copper wires. We can send it [energy] to you like a cell [mobile] phone call, where you want it and when you want it, in real time."
Dr. Neville Marzwell, technical manager, Advanced Concepts and Technology Innovations program, NASA's Jet Propulsion Laboratory, 2005

This technician is assembling photovoltaic solar panels into modules.

Transmitting microwaves is hazardous because microwave radiation is dangerous to health. But some of the risk could be avoided by placing the receivers in remote locations such as deserts.

As technology improves, the cost of launching, assembling, and maintaining such a system will probably come down. Other countries are interested in space solar power. The Japanese Ministry of Economy, Trade, and Industry has published plans to have a solar power station in operation by 2040.

HOW DOES A PV CELL WORK?

A PV cell is made of thin layers of silicon, each connected to an electrical circuit. The silicon is covered by glass, or some other transparent material, and sealed. When light strikes the silicon, the electrons get excited and move between the layers, producing an electric current. The more light there is, the more electrons move around, and the greater the current that is produced.

Individual cells can vary in size, from about half an inch (1 centimeter) to about 4 inches (10 centimeters) across. However, each cell only produces 1 or 2 watts, which is not enough to power most appliances. A number of cells are therefore connected together in a sealed casing called a module. To generate even more power, the modules can be connected together to create an array.

Water Power

Water power, in the form of simple water wheels, has been used for thousands of years. Unlike wind power and solar energy, water power already supplies about 20 percent of the world's electricity. But wind, solar, and water power all have the potential to supply much more.

Water wheel design

There are three types of water wheel: the undershot, overshot, and horizontal wheel. The undershot wheel spins when flowing water hits it from the bottom. The overshot water wheel has been used in Europe for over 2,000 years. This type of wheel is far more efficient, as the water falls onto the wheel from above. Both the weight and force of the water cause the wheel to turn.

This diagram shows how an overshot water wheel works.

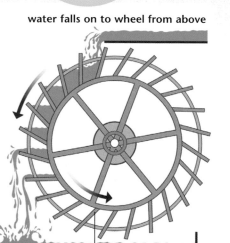

water falls on to wheel from above

force of water spins the wheel

The horizontal wheel has vanes sticking out from a wooden pole. A jet of water directed onto the vanes turns the wheel. This is not as powerful as a vertical wheel. Horizontal wheels were common in ancient China. They have also been used to turn millstones, to grind grain into flour.

Generating electricity

A major breakthrough came when engineers worked out how to use the energy from a water wheel to generate electricity. They invented the water **turbine**, which uses swirling water to spin a **rotor**. The rotor is connected to a generator to produce electricity. This design is very similar to a wind turbine, in which the rotor is spun by wind.

Between 1820 and 1850, engineers came up with several designs known as reactive water turbines, in which the turbine was inside a casing. In these, the flowing water was directed into the turbine, to push on the blades and cause them to spin. One of the most efficient was the Francis turbine, designed by James Francis, a British-born engineer working in the United States.

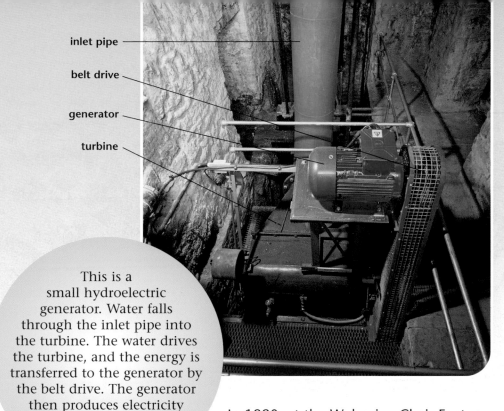

inlet pipe

belt drive

generator

turbine

This is a small hydroelectric generator. Water falls through the inlet pipe into the turbine. The water drives the turbine, and the energy is transferred to the generator by the belt drive. The generator then produces electricity for about 15 homes.

In 1880, at the Wolverine Chair Factory in Grand Rapids, Michigan, 16 lamps were powered using a water turbine. Two years later, the first hydroelectric power plant in the United States was built on the Fox River in Wisconsin. A water wheel was placed under a 10-foot (3-meter) fall of water. This generated 12.5 **kilowatts** of electricity, which powered all the machinery in the local paper mill.

HOW IS HYDROELECTRIC POWER GENERATED?

A hydroelectric power plant converts the energy of flowing water into electricity. The amount of electricity generated depends on the volume of water and the head of the water (the height the water falls). The head can be increased by placing the turbines in the bottom of a dam. The dam creates a lake or reservoir, in which the water is stored. When gates are opened, the water flows through pipes, known as **penstocks**, to the power room. There, the jet of water strikes the turbine blades. The kinetic (movement) energy of the water is changed into mechanical energy. The spinning turbines generate electricity.

Lester Pelton, ingenious inventor

During the 1870s in the United States, gold miners used a lot of machinery powered by steam engines, which needed a constant supply of wood or coal. An inventor named Lester Pelton (1829–1908) traveled to California during the Gold Rush and saw an opportunity.

Lester Pelton devised the Pelton Runner, which has divided buckets along its outer edge. His design is still in use today.

Pelton knew that there were plenty of fast-flowing streams in the area. In 1877, he designed a water wheel that could generate electricity using a jet of water. The water was directed onto a double-bucketed wheel, causing it to move. His design, called the Pelton Runner, was far more efficient than reactive turbines. It was first used to power machinery at the Mayflower Mine in California, in 1878.

Long-distance electricity

During the early 1880s, electricity from water power could only power industries and homes that were close to the plant. However, in 1887 electricity companies switched from **direct current (DC) to alternating current (AC)**, which was more efficient. Less electricity was therefore lost as it passed along the wires, and electricity could now be transmitted over long distances. By the 1940s, 40 percent of U.S. electricity was generated by hydroelectric power.

Large hydroelectric dams

The first hydroelectric power stations were built beside rivers and relied on the river flow as their power source. However, in the early 1900s engineers realized that they could get a bigger head of water by placing water turbines at the bottom of a dam.

Until this point, dams had been built across rivers to create reservoirs. The reservoir would be used to supply cities with water and to irrigate crops. Dams were also used to control the flow of water down the river. Now they had an additional purpose. They could also be used to generate electricity.

Larger dams were needed to create a bigger head of water, in order to generate more electricity. But the dams needed to be able to withstand the huge pressure of the water in the reservoirs. Dams made from earth were not strong enough. Reinforced concrete, which contains steel to increase its strength, was the answer.

One of the first dams to be built using reinforced concrete was Hoover Dam, on the Colorado River.

THAT'S AMAZING!

Construction of Hoover Dam started in 1931, under the supervision of chief engineer Frank Crowe. Concrete can be very tricky to use because it releases heat as it solidifies. The foundations were so deep that the concrete had to be added gradually, in layers. If the concrete had been poured in all at once, the dam would have cracked.

The generators at Hoover Dam began transmitting electricity in October 1936. Today, there are 17 large turbines that generate a maximum of about 2,000 megawatts of hydroelectric power.

The world's largest hydroelectric dams

Since the 1930s, many large hydroelectric dams have been built around the world, dwarfing Hoover Dam. The largest, Three Gorges Dam in China, is currently under construction.

Name	Location	Date constructed	Maximum electricity generation (in megawatts)
Grand Coulee	United States	1942–1980	6,809
Itaipu	Brazil–Paraguay border	1984–1991	12,666
Guri	Venezuela	1986	10,200
Three Gorges	China	Due to finish 2009	18,200

When it is finished in 2009, Three Gorges Dam in China will generate about 12 percent of the country's electricity. The dam will be 1.2 miles (2 kilometers) long and 606 feet (185 meters) high.

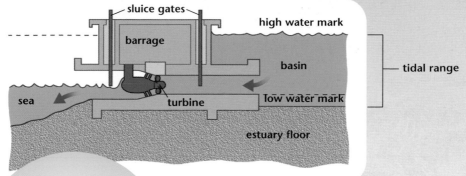

This diagram shows a cross-section of a tidal barrage. The turbines are positioned at the bottom of the barrage. When the tide goes out, water rushes through the turbines and out to sea.

Tidal barrages

It is not just rivers that can be used to generate electricity. The power of the tides can also be harnessed. **Tidal barrages** are dams across estuaries or small basins. Their use dates back to 1008, when a tidal barrage is said to have been built in Venice, Italy. The early tidal barrages were used to grind grain. Small dams with swinging gates were built across tidal basins. When the tide came in, the water pushed the gates open and flowed into the area behind the dam. When the tide turned, the gates shut, and water was forced through a water wheel. But power was only available for two to three hours a day.

THAT'S AMAZING!

On the Severn Estuary in the United Kingdom, there is a tidal range of more than 39 feet (12 meters). A proposed tidal barrage here could generate about 12 percent of the country's electricity. But this is still only a proposal.

Modern tidal barrages are based on the same principles. However, in order to be efficient, they need to be built on estuaries with a **tidal range** of at least 16 feet (5 meters). In 1960, construction of the first commercial tidal barrage started on the Rance River, in France. Inside the barrage are 24 highly efficient turbines, which generate electricity when the tide is flowing both in and out. About 480 **gigawatt** hours of electricity are generated each year, enough to power about 200,000 homes.

The second commercial tidal barrage was constructed at Annapolis Royale, Nova Scotia, Canada, in 1982. There are another 10 small barrages elsewhere in the world.

Getting energy from waves

It is not just flowing water that can be harnessed for energy. Energy can also be generated from waves. However, there was very little interest in investing in wave power research until the price of oil soared during the 1970s. Several governments, including those of the United Kingdom, Japan, and Norway, have since sponsored wave power research programes.

Harnessing wave power was a great technical challenge, and researchers had little background information to draw upon. They needed to know about oceanography, engineering, and fluid mechanics (the study of flowing fluids). It has proved difficult to harness wave energy and convert it into electricity on a large enough scale to be worthwhile. In the 1970s, researchers concentrated on two types of wave power generation device: shore-based and floating.

Limpet 500, the world's first commercial-scale wave power station, lies on the coast of Islay, a Scottish Hebridean island. It generates 500 kilowatts of electricity—enough to power 300 homes.

Shore-based wave power devices

One of the most successful wave machines is the Land Installed Marine Powered Energy Transformer, known as the Limpet. It was developed in 1992 by Professor Alan Wells of Queen's University, Belfast, Ireland. The Limpet is a very simple machine. Waves crashing onto the machine force a column of air through the turbines, and this generates electricity. Their prototype was built on the shore of the Scottish Island of Islay. An improved Limpet was built in 2000, and it produces electricity for the local village.

A new wave power station based on the Limpet is being built in the Danish Faroe Islands. This one has a tunnel cut into the base of the cliff. Water rushes through the tunnel into the chamber where the turbines are located. This new design is well-protected and unobtrusive, and therefore ideal for protected coastlines.

Floating wave power devices

Floating wave power machines have proved to be particularly challenging. There have been problems with securing the devices and transmitting the electricity to the shore. They are also more difficult to maintain.

One of the first floating devices, built during the 1970s, was the Salter's Duck, named after its inventor, Stephen Salter. The original design used clam shapes, which rotated around an axle, or spine. The "clams" were moved by the waves, and this generated electricity. The latest version of the Duck has dozens of **pistons** inside a cylinder. As the Duck bobs up and down on the water, the pistons are pushed in and out. This movement generates electricity.

This photograph shows a scale model of the Salter's Duck being tested in a wave tank at Edinburgh University, in Scotland. Waves generated on the right have their energy almost totally absorbed by the Duck, leaving calm water behind (left).

Small is better

Most of the wave projects of the 1970s failed because investors did not believe they would be commercially viable. However, since the 1990s some innovative engineering companies have designed small-scale wave machines, which are suitable for powering remote coastal communities. The engineers have gained from the experience of the oil industry in building offshore oil and gas platforms.

The United States and Japan have some wave energy projects, but Europe leads the way in this field. The new generation of wave machines produce no more than 2 megawatts of energy each. One of the devices, Pelamis, is a raft converter, which has undergone tests off the coast of Scotland. Raft converters are made up of sections that are hinged together to create a large raft-like structure. As waves pass underneath the sections, they flex up and down, a lot like a train going over hills. The energy from the raft's movement is used to generate electricity. Pelamis can produce about 750 kilowatts of electricity (enough to power around 500 homes).

This photograph shows Pelamis undergoing sea trials.

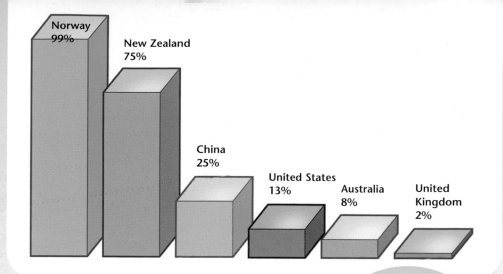

Norway
99%

New Zealand
75%

China
25%

United States
13%

Australia
8%

United Kingdom
2%

The future of water power

If every possible hydroelectric site in the world were used, 80 percent of the world's electricity could be generated. However, this is unlikely to happen. Most of the remaining sites are in the developing world, where the cost of building dams would be very high because there are few good roads and there is no electricity distribution grid. Some are located in earthquake-prone areas, and others are in areas of political unrest. Building more large hydroelectric plants would also have some major environmental consequences, such as the flooding of river valleys to create reservoirs and the creation of barriers that would stop fish from moving along rivers.

In 2005, hydroelectric power supplied about 20 percent of the world's electricity. In some countries, hydroelectric power supplies virtually all the electricity.

Engineers are now looking at ways of generating more electricity from the existing plants, for example by installing computerized control systems and improved turbines. In addition, some of the surplus electricity generated during periods of low demand could be used to produce hydrogen for use in **fuel cells** (see pages 50–55).

Another approach is to look at projects that can generate electricity for a small community. These cause less environmental damage and are easy to build. New turbines that can work efficiently with a small head of water are being developed. There are also plans to redevelop some of the small hydroelectric sites that were abandoned during the 1950s and 1960s, when oil and coal were cheap.

Nuclear Energy

The amount of electricity generated using solar, wind, and water power will not be enough to meet demand in the future. Another source of energy is nuclear power.

Atomic structure

During the 1800s, scientists made discoveries about the atom's structure that eventually led to the development of nuclear energy. In 1897, British scientist J.J. Thomson (1856–1940) proved that there were tiny particles, called **electrons**, in the atom. According to his model of the atom, the electrons were buried randomly in a sphere of positive charges (later identified as **protons**). This theory was not correct. However, it was an important step because it helped Thomson's student Ernest Rutherford (1871–1937) to discover the real structure of atoms.

Ernest Rutherford carried out much of his pioneering research on atomic structure at the University of Manchester in England.

Rutherford had seen Thomson's experiments and decided to carry out some experiments of his own. The breakthrough came 10 years later. Two of Rutherford's students, Hans Geiger and Ernest Marsden, fired positively charged alpha particles (made of two protons and two **neutrons**) through incredibly thin sheets of gold foil. A screen was placed behind the foil. Any particles passing through the foil would show up as flashes of light on the screen. This way, the students could figure out how many particles passed through the foil and how many were deflected. Any deflections were caused by alpha particles bumping into positive particles in the atom. They found that most of the particles passed straight through the foil and very few were deflected.

Rutherford concluded that most of the atom must be made up of empty space. If the positively charged particles had existed throughout the atom, as suggested by Thomson, more of the particles would have been deflected.

In 1911, Rutherford published his atomic theory. He likened the atom to a miniature solar system, with a **nucleus** at its center and electrons rotating around it.

Ernest Rutherford's most famous achievement was to "split the atom." He fired alpha particles into nitrogen. This sometimes caused a tiny part of the nucleus to break away. In 1920, he identified the part that broke away as the proton. It had a positive charge.

Rutherford knew that electrons orbited the atom's nucleus. But he had not yet discovered that the nucleus contained neutrons as well as protons.

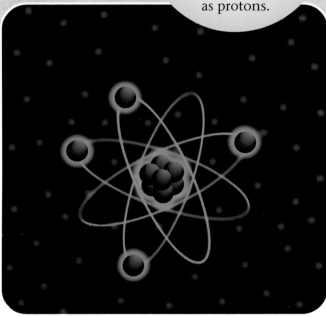

? WHAT ARE ATOMS, ELEMENTS, AND ISOTOPES?

An atom contains protons, neutrons, and electrons. The protons and neutrons are found in the central nucleus. The electrons form a cloud around the nucleus. Each type of atom has a specific number of protons, neutrons, and electrons. There are always equal numbers of positively charged protons and negatively charged electrons, so an atom has no charge. For example, an oxygen atom contains 8 protons, 8 neutrons, and 8 electrons.

An element is a substance, such as oxygen or nitrogen, that contains one type of atom. Sometimes two atoms of the same element have different numbers of neutrons. These atoms are then called isotopes.

Explosive neutrons

The neutron, the third type of particle in the atom's nucleus, was discovered in 1932, by English scientist James Chadwick (1891–1974). Then, in 1934, Italian scientist Enrico Fermi (1901–1954) showed that neutrons could split atoms. When Fermi bombarded uranium with neutrons, he caused an explosive reaction and created **elements** that were much lighter than uranium. He had carried out atomic **fission**, although he did not realize it at the time.

In 1939, Otto Hahn and Fritz Strassman, in Germany, proved that uranium could be split to form much lighter elements, such as barium. But the mass of the new elements was a little less than the mass of the original element. The only explanation was that some of the atoms' mass had been converted into heat energy. This was a key step toward developing nuclear energy.

This is an artist's impression of scientists observing the first controlled chain reaction at Chicago Pile 1 in 1942. No photographs could be taken because the radiation affected the photographic film.

Atomic chain reactions

Danish scientist Niels Bohr (1885–1962) found that fission would not take place in natural uranium. It would only take place in a rare isotope called uranium-235.

He also discovered that neutrons both caused fission and were produced by it. This gave him the exciting idea of a chain reaction. The neutrons produced in the first fission reaction could cause more fission reactions. These reactions would produce more neutrons, and so on.

In 1939, Bohr traveled to the United States, where he discussed his chain reaction idea with Enrico Fermi. By 1941, Fermi and his associate Leo Szilard had drawn up plans for a uranium chain reactor. In 1942, Fermi's team started work under a disused sports stadium in Chicago, Illinois. They built a reactor called Chicago Pile 1.

The reactor contained rods of uranium within a stack of graphite (a type of carbon). The graphite stopped the neutrons from escaping. The reaction was controlled by cadmium rods. When the rods were lowered into the pile, they absorbed the neutrons and slowed the chain reaction. When the rods were raised out of the pile, more neutrons were available to split atoms, and the chain reaction got faster.

On December 2, 1942, the first demonstration took place. The control rods were raised and nuclear fission reactions started. Within a few hours, the chain reaction was underway. The world had entered the nuclear age.

WHERE DOES ATOMIC ENERGY COME FROM?

Atoms may be tiny, but there is a large amount of energy holding the nucleus together. The nuclei of atoms can be split, in a process called fission. This causes the release of energy, in the form of heat and radiation. The heat can generate electricity in a power station.

Nuclear power plants

Nuclear power stations generate electricity like any other power station. The energy created heats water, and steam from the boiling water turns turbines, generating electricity. After World War Two ended in 1945 with the devastation caused by atomic bomb blasts in the Japanese cities of Hiroshima and Nagasaki, the U.S. government encouraged the development of nuclear energy for peaceful purposes.

The first electricity from nuclear energy was generated in December 1951. In 1954, the world's first commercial nuclear power station, using a water-cooled reactor, opened at Obninsk, Russia. It was followed in 1956 by a gas-cooled reactor at Calder Hall in England. Then, in 1957, the Shippingport Reactor, a pressurized-water reactor, opened in the United States.

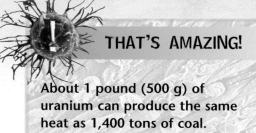

THAT'S AMAZING!

About 1 pound (500 g) of uranium can produce the same heat as 1,400 tons of coal.

There are several different types of nuclear power station. They use different moderators (to slow the neutrons down) and coolants (to stop the reactor from overheating). The most common design is the pressurized-water reactor, in which the coolant and moderator is water under high pressure. These reactors are considered the safest and most reliable.

Most English reactors are gas-cooled reactors with a graphite moderator and carbon dioxide coolant. They also have an excellent safety record. The liquid metal fast-breeder reactor uses either liquid sodium or lead as a coolant, and it has no moderator. There are some other designs, which are still at an experimental stage.

Nuclear energy—a green fuel?

During the 1960s, the nuclear power industry grew rapidly, particularly in the United States. It was seen as economical, environmentally clean, and safe. However, during the 1970s and 1980s, concern grew over issues such as reactor safety and how to dispose of radioactive waste.

In 2005, the United States had over 100 nuclear reactors. This is the San Onofre nuclear power plant in California.

Accidents at nuclear power stations, such as Three Mile Island in the United States in 1979 and at Chernobyl in Ukraine in 1986, further dented the public's confidence in nuclear fuel. However, the world is still dependent on nuclear energy. In 2005, there were about 440 commercial nuclear power stations in 31 countries, with a combined capacity of more than 366 **gigawatts**. They supply about 16 percent of the world's electricity. France and Lithuania get more than 75 percent of their electricity from nuclear power.

There is a renewed interest in nuclear power, as countries try to reduce their carbon dioxide **emissions**. About 30 nuclear power stations are being built, and a further 35 are being planned. In addition, many existing power stations have been upgraded to work more efficiently. Nuclear power could be the most environmentally friendly way of producing electricity. But the problem of radioactive waste disposal still needs to be solved. It could be buried underground, where it would have to be stored for hundreds of years until it was safe.

Geothermal Energy

Another potential source of energy is geothermal energy (heat from underground). Around the world, there are hot springs and geysers, where hot water and steam pour out of the ground. This source of heat has long been used by people for cooking, bathing, and heating their homes. For example, the ancient Romans used hot water from the ground to heat their homes in Pompeii. Now geothermal energy can be harnessed to generate electricity.

Naturally occurring steam was first used to generate electricity around 100 years ago at Larderello, Italy. Steam coming out of the ground was piped to a steam **turbine** and used to power a generator. In 1911, the world's first geothermal plant was built nearby in Valle del Diavolo ("Devil's Valley"). Now this area produces 10 percent of the world's geothermal electricity and provides power for about 1 million homes. This is one of the few places in the world where hot granite rocks lie very close to the surface, so the steam emerges at about 430 °Fahrenheit (220 °Celsius). This is high enough to generate electricity.

Larderello, Italy, is one of two locations in the world where high-temperature geothermal steam can be directly used to turn electricity turbines. Here, steam is shown escaping into a field from an underground source in Larderello.

WHERE DOES GEOTHERMAL HEAT COME FROM?

Almost 4,000 miles (6,500 kilometers) beneath Earth's surface lies the planet's core, where temperatures reach about 10,800 °Fahrenheit (6,000 °Celsius). The core is surrounded by the **mantle**, a layer of rock and **magma** (molten rock). The crust is the outermost layer, made up of large plates that float on the mantle. Magma comes close to the surface in places where the crust is very thin, where there are cracks, and in volcanic regions. The magma heats up underground water.

In 1921, John Grant started work on a similar geothermal power plant at the Geysers, a hot springs and popular tourist resort in northern California. Grant believed that there was an underground reservoir of steam, which he could reach by drilling a deep well. His first well was unsuccessful. However, the following year he drilled several successful wells, and he was able to pipe steam straight to the turbines. Soon electricity was being generated to light the buildings and streets. Although there were plans to enlarge the plant, they were never implemented. This was because the pipes and turbines used at the time could not withstand the corrosion caused by impurities in the steam.

In 1960, new wells were dug to reach a steam reservoir more than 1,300 feet (400 meters) down, and a new geothermal power plant was built. This plant, called Magma Power, generated 11 **megawatts** of electricity, and it is still in operation.

The Tatio geyser field lies in the Atacama Desert of northern Chile. It is the largest area of thermal activity in the southern hemisphere.

Hot water reservoirs

The dry steam reservoirs of Larderello and the Geysers are very rare. More common are hot water reservoirs, where the rocks are saturated with hot water. The water is under pressure from the overlying rocks and it cannot turn into steam. To generate electricity, the hot water, at temperatures of 300–750 °Fahrenheit (150–400 °Celsius), is piped to a power plant. At the plant, the pressure is lowered, and the water instantly changes into steam. These are called flash power plants.

During the 1980s, improvements were made so that the plants could use water at a temperature of 250–390 °Fahrenheit (120–200 °Celsius). This was not hot enough to flash into steam. These were called binary cycle power plants. The hot water was piped into a heat exchanger (see page 17).

The first flash power plant, shown here, was developed at Wairakei, in New Zealand, in the 1950s.

In the heat exchanger, the heat transferred to another liquid, which vaporized when it was heated. The vapor was used to power the turbine. Afterward, the vapor was **condensed** back into a liquid and reheated again.

Ground heat

The heat just below the surface of the ground can also be utilized. In 1948, Professor Carl Nielsen of Ohio State University developed the first ground source heat pump to heat his house. He knew that the temperature of the ground about 3 feet (1 meter) below the surface was always 45–59 °Fahrenheit (7–15 °Celsius). He buried pipes in the ground and circulated water through them. Heat from the ground was transferred to the water, and this was piped into the house. This system has now been adapted for use around the world. In the United States alone, there are more than 300,000 buildings using this type of pump.

The future of geothermal power

In 2000, geothermal energy generated more than 7,000 megawatts of power in 21 countries. The United States produces about 2,700 megawatts of electricity from geothermal energy, which is comparable to burning 60 million barrels of oil. In countries with no natural oil and coal reserves, such as Iceland, Kenya, and New Zealand, geothermal power is a major energy source. For example, in Kenya, there are three plants at Olkaria, and production is to be increased by about 580 megawatts. Geothermal power will then supply 25 percent of Kenya's electricity. Another area that may one day be explored is the drilling of wells deep into magma to access the extra-high temperatures.

WILL GEOTHERMAL POWER RUN OUT?

Although geothermal sites can provide heat for many decades, they eventually get used up, as the water is extracted and the ground cools. For example, in Larderello, Italy, steam pressure levels have dropped by 30 percent since the 1950s.

Biopower

A huge potential source of alternative energy is biopower (power from plants). Plants can harness the sun's energy because their leaves contain a green pigment called chlorophyll. This pigment enables plants to use light to combine carbon dioxide and water in order to make sugars. The plants use these sugars to fuel their growth and reproduction. People have cut down trees and used their wood as an energy source for thousands of years. But there are other plants that could be just as useful. Technology is making it possible for us to access this type of energy.

This villager in Haryana State, India, fuels her biogas stove with methane produced by manure from her farm animals. The manure is collected in a pit, and the methane is piped to the house.

Biofuels

Many plants can be grown for fuel. These **biofuels** are mostly fast-growing species, such as willow and sugar cane. Plant wastes, such as straw, are just as valuable. However, biofuels tend to be bulky, so they are more difficult to transport and handle. There is also the problem of **emissions**. Modern power stations have a filter in their chimneys, to remove harmful emissions produced by the burning fuel. When biofuels are burned, the filter may have to be modified. However, these problems can be overcome.

THAT'S AMAZING!

The food company Quaker Oats has teamed up with the University of Iowa to develop a way of burning the huge quantities of waste oat hulls produced by the company each day. The oat hulls will replace some of the coal that is burned at a nearby power station.

Biogas

When animal and plant wastes are decomposed by bacteria in an anaerobic (oxygen-free) environment, they release a mixture of gases, particularly **methane**. This source of methane is renewable. There are many ways in which methane can be generated. For instance, in landfill sites the **organic** matter in household waste rots and produces methane. This can be collected, using pipes, and burned to generate electricity.

In India, organic waste is often placed in pits under the ground. There, the waste rots and releases **biogas** (a mixture of methane and carbon dioxide). The methane is used as a fuel for cooking and heating. For a long time, these underground pits only generated enough biogas for a family or a small community. Now industrial-scale biogas plants are being built to deal with much larger quantities of waste.

Similar biogas plants have been built in Europe, especially in Germany, Denmark, and the Netherlands, to deal with large quantities of animal waste and surplus fruit and vegetables. All sorts of waste could be treated in this way, including organic waste from pulp and paper industries and waste water from sugar refineries and tanning factories.

This is a biogas plant in Montreal, Canada. Some of the latest biogas plants generate methane from animal waste, especially waste from pigs and cows.

Fuel for cars

Today, most cars are powered by gasoline or diesel fuels, which are obtained from crude oil. However, this has not always been the case. In 1807, Swiss inventor François Isaac de Rivaz (1752–1828) made an internal combustion engine that was fueled by a mixture of hydrogen and oxygen. There were steam-powered engines too. Then, in 1893, German inventor Rudolf Diesel (1858–1913) designed a new style of engine that could run on vegetable oil. This engine was named the diesel engine, and it was used to power cars.

However, as oil companies got larger and more powerful, they wanted cars to be fueled by their diesel fuel, rather than vegetable oils from farmers. During the 1920s, they altered the design of the diesel engine slightly, so that it could run on their diesel fuel. The alternative fuels were forgotten or ignored.

The oil from sunflower seeds has been used in cooking for hundreds of years, but it can also be used to fuel cars.

When the price of oil increased in the 1970s, many people looked for alternative fuels to power their vehicles. One such fuel is **ethanol**, a type of alcohol made from maize, sugar cane, and even organic waste material such as straw. In Brazil, farmers were encouraged to grow sugar cane, which was used to make ethanol. Soon, millions of cars in North and South America were being powered by alcohol-based fuels. Ethanol has seen a revival in the United States too, which has some of the world's toughest vehicle emission controls. Now, some car manufacturers are making "flexible-fuel vehicles" that can run on ethanol or gasoline.

A worker tests a sample of alcohol at an alcohol distillery in Sao Paulo, Brazil. The use of alcohol fuel in cars is increasing because oil prices have risen and governments are encouraging people to use less polluting alternative fuels.

Biodiesel

Biodiesel can run in diesel engines with little modification. It can be made from waste cooking oil or from the oil extracted from certain crops. These crops include oil seed rape, sunflower, and palm oil. Biodiesel is a cleaner fuel than diesel, as it produces less carbon dioxide. Since 1991, biodiesel plants have spread through Europe. Most diesel fuels now contain 5 percent biodiesel. Biodiesel helps to combat **global warming** because it is a "carbon neutral" fuel. Plants take up carbon dioxide when they are photosynthesizing, and this carbon dioxide is released when the oil is burned in the car. Fossil fuels, such as coal, were also formed as a result of photosynthesis. But when fossil fuels are burned, they release carbon dioxide that has remained locked up in the fuels for millions of years.

Fuel Cells

The **fuel cell** promises to be an important power source in the future. But its origins go back to 1839 when William Grove (1811–1896), a British scientist, was working on batteries. He knew that oxygen and hydrogen gas were produced when an electric current was passed through water (in a process called **electrolysis**). He wondered whether he could reverse this process and make electricity by combining oxygen and hydrogen.

Grove took two platinum **electrodes**. The end of the first electrode was sealed in a tube of oxygen gas. The end of the second electrode was sealed in a tube of hydrogen gas. When he dipped the other ends of the electrodes in a container of dilute sulphuric **acid**, a small electric current began to flow between them. If he joined up several of these devices, he could produce a larger current. He called his device a "gas battery." He thought it could one day replace coal as an energy source. But there was little interest in his invention at the time, so he did not develop the idea any further. His battery was the world's first fuel cell, although this term was not used until 1889 by two chemists named Ludwig Mond and Charles Langer.

These hydrogen fuel cells use hydrogen and oxygen from air to generate electricity. They have no moving parts, nor do they need to be recharged like a battery.

This London bus is powered by a fuel cell that runs on hydrogen gas.

THAT'S AMAZING!

In 1959, Harry Karl Ihrig, a manufacturer of farm equipment, demonstrated his 20-**horsepower** tractor, powered by fuel cells. He had created a stack of 1,008 fuel cells to generate about 15 kilowatts of electricity. Although the design was not very practical, it proved for the first time that fuel cells could generate enough electricity to power a vehicle.

The alkaline fuel cell

Francis Bacon (1904–1992), a British engineer, wanted to redesign Grove's fuel cell so that it was more practical and could be sold commercially. He replaced the expensive platinum **catalyst** with inexpensive nickel. He also replaced the acid with a weak solution of potassium hydroxide (an **alkali**), so that the metal electrode was not corroded. Another change was the use of a porous electrode with lots of tiny holes. This created more contact between the gases and the catalyst, leading to more reaction and therefore more electricity. However, these fuel cells are very expensive and easily contaminated, so they need a supply of pure hydrogen and oxygen. Producing hydrogen requires a lot of energy (see panel on page 54).

By 1932, Bacon had a working fuel cell. In 1940, he went to King's College, London, to carry out more research. In 1959, he finally presented his Bacon cell. This was a fuel cell that could produce about 5 **kilowatts** of electricity, enough to power a welding machine.

Fuel cells in space

During the 1960s, engineers at NASA were looking for ways of powering the equipment on board the *Apollo* and *Gemini* spacecraft. They considered a number of options, including nuclear-powered batteries and **photovoltaic (PV) cells**, but they decided that fuel cells were perfect for space. Weight for weight, they produced more electricity than a conventional battery. In addition, the reaction between oxygen and hydrogen produced water, which could be used by the astronauts.

The *Apollo* spacecraft carried three hydrogen-oxygen fuel cell stacks in the service module. Each unit weighed about 250 pounds (114 kilograms) and contained 31 fuel cells connected together. It could generate a maximum of about 2.3 kilowatts. These fuel cells proved incredibly reliable and worked for 10,000 hours over 18 missions.

Alkaline fuel cells were also used in the space shuttles. By the 1980s, fuel cell efficiency had improved. Each of the three stacks of fuel cells used in the shuttle generated 12 kilowatts, a considerable improvement on those used in the *Apollo* spacecraft.

The alkaline fuel cell played a vital role in powering equipment on board spacecraft such as *Apollo* and *Gemini*. This is the *Gemini-Titan 4* lift-off in 1965. On board were U.S. astronauts James McDivitt and Ed White.

? HOW DOES A FUEL CELL DIFFER FROM A BATTERY?

A fuel cell works a lot like a conventional battery. It converts the energy released in a chemical reaction into electrical energy. A conventional battery eventually "dies," and either has to be recharged or thrown away. In a fuel cell, there is a continuous supply of reactants, so the fuel cell will never die.

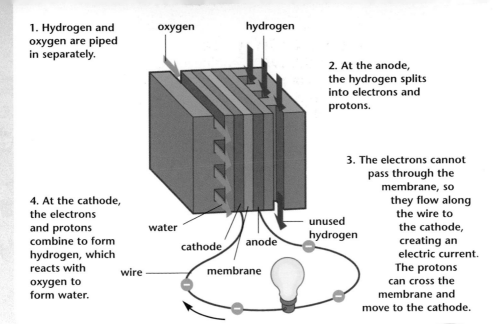

1. Hydrogen and oxygen are piped in separately.

oxygen

hydrogen

2. At the anode, the hydrogen splits into electrons and protons.

3. The electrons cannot pass through the membrane, so they flow along the wire to the cathode, creating an electric current. The protons can cross the membrane and move to the cathode.

4. At the cathode, the electrons and protons combine to form hydrogen, which reacts with oxygen to form water.

water

cathode

anode

unused hydrogen

wire

membrane

This diagram shows how a fuel cell works.

Different types of fuel cell

Over the years, several types of fuel cell have been developed, each suited to a different use. The most common is the hydrogen fuel cell, derived from William Grove's design, which runs on hydrogen and oxygen.

During the late 1930s, Swiss scientists Emil Baur and H. Preis experimented with solid oxide **electrolytes**, rather than liquids. Solid oxide fuel cells use a hard ceramic electrolyte and operate at temperatures up to 1,830 °Fahrenheit (1,000 °Celsius). They are ideal for providing electricity for factories or small communities. The waste heat from the fuel cell can be used to create steam, which can power a **turbine** to generate electricity. This increases the system's efficiency even more. The phosphoric acid fuel cell uses phosphoric acid as the electrolyte. These fuel cells can be used in buildings rather than cars, as they take a while to warm up and start generating electricity. The waste heat can be used to heat water.

The proton exchange membrane (PEM) fuel cell was developed by General Motors during the 1960s. The electrolyte is a membrane (thin, permeable sheet) coated with platinum. These fuel cells are small and light, and they can work at low temperatures. They have been used in cars and buses and to power equipment such as computers.

Powering cars

When an internal combustion engine is converted to run on hydrogen, the efficiency of the engine is more than doubled, from 15–25 percent to almost 60 percent. However, cars can be even more efficient if the engine is replaced by a hydrogen fuel cell. In 1991, American Roger Billings and his team built the first car to be powered by a fuel cell. It was called LaserCel 1 and it had a small tank of hydrogen. The hydrogen was piped into the PEM fuel cell, where it reacted with air to generate electricity. The only waste product was water.

However, there are still some hurdles that need to be overcome before cars powered by fuel cells can be mass-produced. The fuel cell has to be reliable and strong enough to be bounced around. It needs to work at both low and high temperatures. It also has to be cheap. At present, most fuel cells have an expensive platinum catalyst, which is easily contaminated by impurities in the hydrogen. But a new nickel-tin catalyst has recently been developed, and this is much cheaper.

Storage devices

There are many potential uses for hydrogen fuel cells. One of the best ones utilizes off-peak electricity, as power companies often have problems matching electricity supply with demand.

? HOW CAN HYDROGEN BE PRODUCED ON A LARGE SCALE?

Most of the current ways of making hydrogen involve the use of gases such as **methane**. They also require electricity, most of which is generated in fossil fuel–fired power stations. But in the future renewable energy will provide the electricity. For instance, the United States plans to produce hydrogen using nuclear power stations. With minor modifications, nuclear reactors can produce hydrogen and electricity at the same time. Another method under investigation involves creating hydrogen from sunlight and water, using a metallic catalyst. This would be a very clean and cheap way of producing hydrogen.

For example, very few people need electricity at night. However, the spare electricity generated at night could be used to make hydrogen. The fuel cells would then use the hydrogen to provide additional electricity during periods of peak demand.

Self-sufficiency in the future

Looking further into the future, every building could have its own fuel cell. The hydrogen would be supplied by underground pipes, in the same way as natural gas is supplied at the moment. Homes could be self-sufficient in energy. Photovoltaic panels on the roof, or a small local wind turbine, could generate enough electricity to produce hydrogen. The hydrogen would be stored near the house for use in the fuel cell, to generate electricity, or power the car. The whole process, from solar panel or wind turbine to fuel cell, could be carried out without producing polluting **greenhouse gases** such as carbon dioxide. No single alternative energy source is likely to supply all our needs. But, taken together, they have the potential to replace fossil fuels.

Car manufacturer General Motors has developed the Hy-wire car, seen here being displayed in China. The Hy-wire car is powered by a hydrogen fuel cell. There are no pedals, brakes, or engine, and the steering wheel has been replaced by a joystick.

Timeline

1767 First solar collector, called a hot box, built by Horace de Saussure.

1789 Uranium discovered by Martin Klaproth.

1839 Photovoltaic effect is discovered by Alexandre-Edmond Becquerel.

1839 First fuel cell built by William Grove.

1860s Auguste Mouchout builds a solar-powered motor.

1877 Water turbine, called the Pelton Runner, designed by Lester Pelton.

1878 Solar power tower built by William Adams.

1880s First parabolic trough, a type of solar reflector, built by John Ericsson.

1882 First hydroelectric plant built on the Fox River, Wisconsin.

1888 Charles F. Brush builds the first windmill to generate electricity.

1891 Clarence Kemp builds the world's first solar water heater.

1897 J.J. Thomson proves that tiny particles called electrons are present in an atom.

1904 First geothermally generated electricity produced at Larderello, Italy.

1911 Ernest Rutherford publishes his theory of atomic structure.

1912 Frank Shuman builds a solar pumping station in Egypt, using parabolic reflectors.

1921 John Grant drills the first well at the Geysers hot springs in California.

1931 G.J.M. Darrieus patents his Vertical Axis Wind Turbine.

1932 Francis Bacon develops an alkaline fuel cell system.

1934 Physicist Enrico Fermi shows that neutrons can split an atom of uranium.

1936 Hoover Dam completed.

1938 Nuclear fission demonstrated by Otto Hahn and Fritz Strassman.

1939 Russell Ohl discovers that a light shining on a crystal of silicon can create an electric current.

1942 Fermi demonstrates the first self-sustaining nuclear chain reaction.

1945 Atomic bombs dropped on Hiroshima and Nagasaki, Japan.

1948 Professor Carl Nielsen uses ground heat to heat his home.

1951 First nuclear power produced at Experimental Breeder Reactor I in Arco, Idaho.

1954 First commercial nuclear power plant built at Obninsk, Russia.

1956–1957 Danish engineer Johannes Juul designs the Gedser wind turbine.

1959 Francis Bacon demonstrates his fuel cell.

1959 Harry Karl Ihrig produces a fuel cell that can power a tractor.

1960s Fuel cells used in the Apollo space program.

1960 Work begins on the La Rance tidal barrage in France.

1969 Solar furnace built at Odeillo, France.

1973 Oil crisis starts in October.

1979 Nuclear accident at Three Mile Island nuclear power station, Pennsylvania.

1986 Major nuclear accident at Chernobyl nuclear power station in Ukraine.

1991 First commercial offshore wind farm built off the coast of Denmark.

1991 Roger Billings and his team produce the first fuel cell-powered car.

1992 Limpet wave power machine developed by Professor Alan Wells and his team at Wavegen.

2000 Improved Limpet built on the Scottish island of Islay.

2000 Daimler-Chrysler begins to deliver 30 hydrogen fuel cell-powered buses to European bus operators.

2002 General Motors unveils the Hy-wire car, which is powered by a fuel cell.

Biographies

These are some of the leading scientists in the story of alternative energy.

Francis Bacon (1904–1992)

Francis Bacon was born in 1904, in Essex, England. He was educated at Eton College and then Cambridge University. After college he worked for an electrical company and became interested in developing fuel cells. He modified William Grove's design to create his own alkaline fuel cells. He continued to modify his design until he successfully demonstrated a working fuel cell in 1959. His fuel cells were used in the U.S. space program during the 1960s. He worked as an energy consultant until the mid-1970s. In 1991, he was awarded the first Grove Medal.

Roger Billings (1948–)

Roger Billings was born in Provo, Utah. In 1965, while still at high school, he devised a way of powering a Ford Model-A truck using hydrogen gas. He studied at Brigham Young University, where he was awarded a research grant by the Ford Motor Company to carry out research into hydrogen as a fuel for cars. During the 1980s, he received government grants to continue his research. In 1991, he produced the world's first fuel cell car. Billings has also been very successful in business. During the 1970s, he set up a number of companies that carried out research in computing. The companies built one of the world's first personal computers, invented the double-sided floppy disk drive, and invented a method of sharing information between personal computers over a network.

Enrico Fermi (1901–1954)

Enrico Fermi was born in Rome, Italy, where he attended a local grammar school. In 1918, he was awarded a fellowship to study at the University of Pisa. He spent the next few years researching mathematical physics. In 1927, Fermi was professor of theoretical physics at the University of Rome, where he carried out research into nuclear fission. In 1938, he emigrated to the United States, where he was professor of physics at Columbia University, in New York. In the same year, he was awarded the Nobel Prize for Physics. After meeting Niels Bohr in 1941, he started work on designs for a nuclear reactor. He became a U.S. citizen in 1944. In 1946, he became a professor at the Institute for Nuclear Studies at the University of Chicago, where he remained until his death in 1954.

William Grove (1811–1896)

William Grove was born in Swansea, Wales, United Kingdom. He went to school in Swansea and then went to Oxford University to study law. He worked as a lawyer for several years, but ill-health forced him to change careers and he decided to study science. In 1839, he invented the first fuel cell. He had a distinguished scientific career. He became a Fellow of the Royal Society and was awarded their medal in 1847. He served as President of the British Association for the Advancement of Science, before returning to law. In 1871, he was made a judge, and he was knighted in 1872. He died in London in 1896.

Lester Pelton (1829–1908)

Lester Pelton is considered to be the father of modern hydroelectric power. He was born in Ohio. When he was 20 years old, he joined the Gold Rush and traveled to California to dig for gold. His observations of gold mining gave him the idea of building a water wheel that could be used to generate electricity. It was called the Pelton Runner and it was first used in Nevada City, California. He patented his invention in 1889.

Ernest Rutherford (1871–1937)

Ernest Rutherford was born in New Zealand, and came to England on a scholarship. In 1895, he began work at the Cavendish Laboratory at Cambridge University, under the guidance of J.J. Thomson. First he studied radio waves and then he looked at newly discovered X-rays. He moved to Manchester University where, in 1911, he published his theory of atomic structure. In 1912, he worked with Niels Bohr. Together they refined the theory of atomic structure, which has remained virtually unchanged ever since. In 1908, Rutherford was awarded the Nobel Prize for Chemistry.

J.J. Thomson (1856–1940)

Joseph John Thomson (known as J.J.) was born in Manchester, England. He first studied at Owen's College (now Manchester University) and then moved to Cambridge University to study mathematics. There, he became professor of physics and head of the Cavendish Laboratory. In 1897, he proved the existence of the electron, for which he was awarded the Nobel Prize for Physics in 1906.

Glossary

acid chemical substance with a pH less than 7

aerodynamic having a streamlined shape so that air or water flows smoothly over the surface

alkali chemical substance with pH greater than 7, that reacts with and neutralizes an acid, e.g. sodium bicarbonate

alternating current (AC) electrical current that surges rapidly backward and forward in the circuit

biofuel fuel derived from plants (especially trees) and animal wastes

biogas name given to the mixture of gases produced by rotting organic matter. The main component of biogas is methane.

catalyst chemical that enables reactions to take place more readily or at a lower temperature

climate change alteration in weather patterns, caused by global warming

condense change from gas or vapor to liquid

direct current (DC) electrical current in which the electricity flows in one direction in the circuit

electrode conductor (usually a wire or rod) through which electricity enters or leaves a substance

electrolysis process of breaking down a chemical using electricity

electrolyte substance that conducts electricity when molten or in a solution, e.g. acidified water

electron negatively charged particle found in an atom. Electrons circle the nucleus. The flow of electrons creates an electric current.

element substance consisting of a single type of atom. For example, the element oxygen is made up of just oxygen atoms.

emission release of a substance into the environment

ethanol type of alcohol

fission splitting of an atom

fuel cell device that converts energy. For example, electricity and heat are produced when hydrogen and oxygen react together in a hydrogen fuel cell.

gigawatt 1 billion watts

global warming process by which the average surface temperature of Earth is gradually increasing

greenhouse gas gas in Earth's atmosphere that traps heat and keeps the planet warm, e.g. carbon dioxide

heliostat device that tracks the movement of the sun

horsepower unit of the rate of doing work. One horsepower equals about 746 watts.

kilowatt 1,000 watts

magma liquid rock

mantle layer between Earth's crust and Earth's core

megawatt 1 million watts

methane odorless, colorless gas, found in natural gas, released from rotting organic matter. Methane is an important greenhouse gas.

microwave short electromagnetic wave, which is longer than infrared but shorter than a radio wave. Microwaves are used for radar and microwave ovens and for transmitting telephone signals, video signals, and other data.

neutron particle found in an atom that does not have a charge

nucleus central part of an atom, containing protons and neutrons

organic made from living organisms; containing carbon atoms

parabolic trough type of solar reflector with a concave shape

penstock pipe or channel that leads from the wall of a dam to a turbine

photovoltaic (PV) cell solar cell that can convert light energy to electricity

piston rod that moves up and down inside a cylinder

power tower rows of mirrors that reflect light on to a central point

proton positively charged particle found in the nucleus of an atom

rotor rotating part, e.g. the blades of a wind turbine

terrawatt 1×10^{12} watts (W); equivalent to the power available from 1,000 power plants of 1 million kilowatt capacity

tidal barrage dam built across an estuary or tidal pool

tidal range difference in height between high tide and low tide

turbine machine that is used to convert movement energy into mechanical energy

Further Resources

If you have enjoyed this book and want to find out more, you can look at the following books and websites.

Books

Chapman, Stephen. *Energy Essentials: Nuclear Energy.* Chicago: Raintree, 2005.

Morgan, Sally. *Science at the Edge: Alternative Energy Sources.* Chicago: Heinemann Library, 2002.

Oxlade, Chris and Nigel Saunders. *Renewable Energy.* Chicago: Raintree, 2004.

Parker, Steve. *Green Files: Future Power.* Chicago: Heinemann Library, 2003.

Sneddon, Robert. *Essential Energy: Energy Alternatives.* Chicago: Heinemann Library, 2006.

Websites

Energy Investigation Agency www.eia.doe.gov/kids/ energyfacts/index.html
Website providing energy facts and information, history, and energy puzzles.

U.S. Department of Energy www.doc.gov/ forstudentsandkids.htm
Comprehensive website with information on all forms of energy.

Renewable Energy www.renewableenergy.com
Website featuring news stories about energy from around the world.

Energy Resources www.darvill.clara.net/ altenerg/index.htm
Informative website on all forms of energy sources, both fossil fuels and alternative fuels.

Index

64